Free Grace Family Catechism

SHAWN LAZAR

FREE GRACE BOOKS
DENTON, TX

Free Grace Family Catechism

Copyright © 2021 by Shawn Lazar

Lazar, Shawn. 1978–

ISBN 9798549373433

Unless otherwise noted, Scripture taken from the King James Version (public domain) or from the New King James Version®. Copyright © 1982 by Thomas Nelson. Used by permission. All rights reserved.

All rights reserved. No part of this book may be reproduced in any form without the prior permission of the publisher, except as provided by USA copyright law.

For Daphne.

Introduction

Are you raising the next Timothy? Do you know where he learned the Christian faith? Not in Sunday school, Bible college, or seminary. Instead, he learned it from his mother and grandmother:

> I am reminded of your sincere faith, which first lived in your grandmother Lois and in your mother Eunice and, I am persuaded, now lives in you also (1 Tim 1:5 NIV).

Two godly women made sure Timothy would know the Scriptures from childhood:

> from infancy you have known the Holy Scriptures, which are able to make you wise for salvation through faith in Christ Jesus (2 Tim 3:15 NIV).

Their efforts paid off. Timothy grew up to become Paul's missionary companion and had a powerful ministry for the Lord. And it all started at home.

Do you think of your home as a school for learning about Christ?

If not, you should. After all, who else will teach your children about Jesus? Don't depend on Sunday school. Your kids can't grow spiritually with only one hour of instruction per week. They need consistent, daily teaching. Sunday school can *help* you, but it can't *replace* you. Parents are responsible for raising their children in the faith:

> Fathers, do not provoke your children to anger, but bring them up in the discipline and instruction of the Lord (Eph 6:4 NASB).

How can you do that?

Take advantage of their natural curiosity. As you know, children ask questions about everything—*Why am I here? Where did I come from? Who made the animals? What does it mean for something to be right or wrong? What does it mean to die? And what happens after you die?* All of those questions are opportunities to give your children Biblical answers so they can think about the world from a divine perspective.

That's what I try to do with my kids. And it helped.

However, sporadically talking about Jesus wasn't good enough. I wanted to cover the basics of the faith in a more orderly way.

In short, I needed a catechism.

Of course, Christians have been using catechisms for centuries, but I struggled to find one that taught a truly Biblical theology—which I take to be Free Grace theology.

For example, most catechisms either explicitly or implicitly teach that eternal salvation depends on being good. They teach works salvation. By contrast, I wanted my kids to see why salvation is by grace, through faith in Christ, apart from works, for everlasting life that cannot be lost (John 3:16; Eph 2:8-9; Gal 2:16).

I was also dissatisfied by how most catechisms answer their questions in their own words. Instead, I wanted the answers to be Bible verses. That way, my children could learn the faith by memorizing Scripture.

How should you use this catechism? My family reads it during supper. I ask a question and we talk about what it means. So far we've never covered more than two questions at a time. The questions are simple, fit for children. But kids can think very big thoughts and can ask very hard questions! Even if my kids don't memorize every single verse, simply discussing the issues is enormously helpful.

While I wrote this catechism for my family, especially for my children, I thought it might help others, too, such as elders, deacons, and small group leaders who may never have had an overview of Bible truth.

But whoever else it may benefit, my main goal is to help godly families raise the next generation of Timothies.

Shawn Lazar
August 2021

On God

Q1. Who created the universe?
A1. In the beginning God created the heavens and the earth (Genesis 1:1).

Q2. How many gods are there?
A2. Hear, O Israel: The LORD our God is one LORD (Deuteronomy 6:4).

Q3. Are we allowed to worship other gods?
A3. Thou shalt have no other gods before me (Exodus 20:3).

Q4. Whom does our family worship?
A4. "but as for me and my house, we will serve the LORD" (Joshua 14:15).

Q5. Are atheists right to deny God's existence?
A5. The fool has said in his heart, "There is no God." (Psalm 14:1).

Q6. How do we know that God exists?
A6. For since the creation of the world His invisible attributes, that is, His eternal power and divine nature, have been clearly perceived, being understood by what has been made, so that they are without excuse (Romans 1:20 NASB).

Q7. Is God a material thing?
A7. "God is Spirit, and those who worship Him must worship in spirit and truth" (John 4:24).

Q8. How "old" is God?
A8. Before the mountains were brought forth, Or ever You had formed the earth and the world, Even from everlasting to everlasting, You are God (Psalm 90:2).

Q9. Is God good?
A9. Oh, taste and see that the LORD is good; Blessed is the man who trusts in Him! (Psalm 34:8).

Q10. Is God holy?
A10. "Holy, holy, holy is the LORD of hosts; The whole earth is full of His glory!" (Isaiah 6:3b).

Q11. Is God loving?
A11. God is love (1 John 4:8b).

Q12. Can God's character change?
A12. "For I am the LORD, I do not change" (Malachi 3:6a).

Q13. How powerful is God?
A13. Great is our Lord, and of great power: his understanding is infinite (Psalm 147:5).

Q14. Where is God?
A14. "Do I not fill heaven and earth?" says the LORD (Jeremiah 23:24c).

On Jesus

Q15. Where was Jesus born?
A15. Now after Jesus was born in Bethlehem of Judea in the days of Herod the king (Matthew 12:1a).

Q16. Was Jesus' birth miraculous?
A16. "Behold, the virgin shall be with child, and bear a Son, and they shall call His name Immanuel," which is translated, "God with us" (Matthew 1:23).

Q17. What did God send Jesus to do?
A17. "For God so loved the world, that he gave his only begotten Son, that whosoever believeth in him should not perish, but have everlasting life. For God sent not his Son into the world to condemn the world; but that the world through him might be saved" (John 3:16-17).

Q18. Where did Jesus grow up?
A18. So He came to Nazareth, where He had been brought up (Luke 4:16a).

Q19. What did Jesus do for work?

A19. "Is this not the carpenter, the Son of Mary, and brother of James, Joses, Judas, and Simon? And are not His sisters here with us?" (Mark 6:3a).

Q20. Did Jesus sin?
A20. For we do not have a High Priest who cannot sympathize with our weaknesses, but was in all points tempted as we are, yet without sin (Hebrews 4:15).

Q21. How did Jesus die?
A21. "And the Son of man shall be betrayed unto the chief priests and unto the scribes, and they shall condemn him to death, And shall deliver him to the Gentiles to mock, and to scourge, and to crucify him: and the third day he shall rise again" (Matthew 20:18-29).

Q22. Did Jesus stay dead?
A22. For I delivered unto you first of all that which I also received, how that Christ died for our sins according to the scriptures; And that he was buried, and that he rose again the third day according to the scriptures (1 Corinthians 15:3-4).

Q23. How many people saw the risen Jesus?
A23. After that He was seen by over five hundred brethren at once, of whom the greater part remain to the present, but some have fallen asleep (1 Corinthians 15:6).

Q24. Is Jesus a man?

A24. For there is one God and one Mediator between God and men, the Man Christ Jesus (1 Timothy 2:5).

Q25. Was Jesus a spirit or a ghost?
A25. "Behold My hands and My feet, that it is I Myself. Handle Me and see, for a spirit does not have flesh and bones as you see I have" (Luke 24:39).

Q26. Is Jesus an angel?
A26. Having become so much better than the angels, as He has by inheritance obtained a more excellent name than they (Hebrews 1:4).

Q27. Did Jesus create the universe?
A27. For by him were all things created, that are in heaven, and that are in earth, visible and invisible, whether they be thrones, or dominions, or principalities, or powers: all things were created by him, and for him (Colossians 1:16).

Q28. Is Jesus God?
A28. And Thomas answered and said to Him, "My Lord and my God!" (John 20:28).

On the Holy Spirit

Q29. Who is the Holy Spirit?
A29. "But the Helper, the Holy Spirit, whom the Father will send in My name, He will teach you all things, and

bring to your remembrance all things that I said to you" (John 14:26).

Q30. What does the Holy Spirit do for the world?
A30. "And when He has come, He will convict the world of sin, and of righteousness, and of judgment" (John 16:8).

Q31. Where does the Holy Spirit dwell?
A31. Do you not know that you are the temple of God and that the Spirit of God dwells in you? (1 Corinthians 3:16).

Q32. How does the Holy Spirit help you in prayer?
A32. Likewise the Spirit also helps in our weaknesses. For we do not know what we should pray for as we ought, but the Spirit Himself makes intercession for us with groanings which cannot be uttered (Romans 8:26).

Q33. Who leads the children of God?
A33. For as many as are led by the Spirit of God, these are sons of God (Romans 8:14).

Q34. Did the Holy Spirit create the universe?
A34. You send forth Your Spirit, they are created; And You renew the face of the earth (Psalm 104:30)

Q35. Is the Holy Spirit God?
A35. But Peter said, "Ananias, why has Satan filled your heart *to lie to the Holy Spirit* and keep back part of the

price of the land for yourself?...*You have not lied to men but to God*" (Acts 5:3-4).

On Angels and Demons

Q36. What are angels?
A36. Are not all angels ministering spirits sent to serve those who will inherit salvation? (Hebrews 1:14 NIV).

Q37. Who is Satan, otherwise known as the Devil?
A37. "You were an anointed guardian cherub. I placed you; you were on the holy mountain of God; in the midst of the stones of fire you walked" (Ezekiel 28:14 ESV).

Q38. Why did Satan rebel against God?
A38. "Your heart was lifted up because of your beauty; You corrupted your wisdom for the sake of your splendor; I cast you to the ground, I laid you before kings, That they might gaze at you" (Ezekiel 28:17).

Q39. What did Satan want to be?
A39. "For you have said in your heart: 'I will ascend into heaven, I will exalt my throne above the stars of God; I will also sit on the mount of the congregation On the farthest sides of the north; I will ascend above the heights of the clouds, I will be like the Most High'" (Isaiah 14:13-14).

Q40. What is the Devil doing now?
A40. Be sober, be vigilant; because your adversary the devil walks about like a roaring lion, seeking whom he may devour (1 Peter 5:8).

Q41. How should you respond to the Devil?
A41. Therefore submit to God. Resist the devil and he will flee from you (James 4:7).

Q42. What will eventually happen to the Devil?
A42. The devil, who deceived them, was cast into the lake of fire and brimstone where the beast and the false prophet are. And they will be tormented day and night forever and ever (Revelation 20:10).

On Sin

Q43. What is sin?
A43. Whoever commits sin also commits lawlessness, and sin is lawlessness (1 John 3:4).

Q44. Who has sinned?
A44. For all have sinned, and come short of the glory of God (Romans 3:23).

Q45. Is anyone good?
A45. And Jesus said to him, "Why do you call me good? No one is good except God alone" (Mark 10:18 ESV).

Q46. Are you forced to sin?
A46. But each one is tempted when he is drawn away by his own desires and enticed. Then, when desire has conceived, it gives birth to sin; and sin, when it is full-grown, brings forth death (James 1:14-15).

Q47. What happens when you commit sin?
A47. Jesus answered them, "Most assuredly, I say to you, whoever commits sin is a slave of sin" (John 8:34).

Q48. What is the penalty of sin?
A48. For the wages of sin is death (Romans 6:23a).

Q49. What is God's attitude toward sin?
A49. For the wrath of God is revealed from heaven against all ungodliness and unrighteousness of men, who suppress the truth in unrighteousness (Romans 1:18).

Q50. How does Jesus deal with sin?
A50. The next day John saw Jesus coming toward him, and said, "Behold! The Lamb of God who takes away the sin of the world!" (John 1:29).

Q51. How did Jesus take away the sins of the world?
A51. Surely he hath borne our griefs, and carried our sorrows: yet we did esteem him stricken, smitten of God, and afflicted. But he was wounded for our transgressions, he was bruised for our iniquities: the chastisement of our peace was upon him; and with his stripes we are healed (Isaiah 53:4-5).

Q52. Why did Jesus have to shed His blood on the cross?
A52. Without shedding of blood there is no forgiveness (Hebrews 9:22b).

Q53. Did Jesus die on the cross for only *some* people?
A53. And he is the propitiation for our sins: and not for ours only, but also for the sins of the whole world (1 John 2:2).

On Salvation

Q54. Are you saved by doing good works?
A54. For by grace are ye saved through faith; and that not of yourselves: it is the gift of God: Not of works, lest any man should boast (Ephesians 2:8-9).

Q55. Then why did God give us laws?
A55. Therefore by the deeds of the law there shall no flesh be justified in his sight: for by the law is the knowledge of sin (Romans 3:20).

Q56. What does the law teach you about salvation?
A56. Therefore the law was our tutor to bring us to Christ, that we might be justified by faith (Galatians 3:24).

Q57. How can you be saved?
A57. And they said, "Believe on the Lord Jesus Christ, and thou shalt be saved, and thy house" (Acts 16:31).

Q58. What happens if you don't believe?
A58. "He that believeth on him is not condemned: but he that believeth not is condemned already, because he hath not believed in the name of the only begotten Son of God" (John 3:18).

Q59. What does it mean to believe?
A59. He was fully convinced that God is able to do whatever he promises (Romans 4:21 NLT).

Q60. Where do you get faith?
A60. So then faith comes by hearing, and hearing by the word of God (Romans 10:17).

Q61. Whose fault is it if you do not believe?
A61. "But you are not willing to come to Me that you may have life" (John 5:40).

Q62. What kind of life does Jesus give you when you believe?
A62. "He that believeth on the Son hath everlasting life: and he that believeth not the Son shall not see life; but the wrath of God abideth on him" (John 3:36).

Q63. Can a believer ever be condemned?
A63. "Verily, verily, I say unto you, He that heareth my word, and believeth on him that sent me, hath everlasting life, and shall not come into condemnation; but is passed from death unto life" (John 5:24).

Q64. Can anyone take a believer from God's hand?
A64. "And I give unto them eternal life; and they shall never perish, neither shall any man pluck them out of my hand. My Father, which gave them me, is greater than all; and no man is able to pluck them out of my Father's hand" (John 10:28-29).

Q65. Do believers stay dead?
A65. Jesus said to her, "I am the resurrection and the life. He who believes in Me, though he may die, he shall live. And whoever lives and believes in Me shall never die. Do you believe this?" (John 11:25-26).

Q66. Is there any other Savior other than Jesus?
A66. "Neither is there salvation in any other: for there is none other name under heaven given among men, whereby we must be saved" (Acts 4:12).

Q67. Is there any other way of salvation other than Jesus?
A67. Jesus said to him, "I am the way, the truth, and the life. No one comes to the Father except through Me" (John 14:6).

Q68. Where do unbelievers go when they die?
A68. "And being in torments in Hades, he lifted up his eyes and saw Abraham afar off, and Lazarus in his bosom" (Luke 16:23).

Q69. Where will unbelievers spend eternity?

A69. And anyone not found written in the Book of Life was cast into the lake of fire (Revelation 20:15).

Q70. Where do believers go when they die?
A70. We are confident, yes, well pleased rather to be absent from the body and to be present with the Lord (2 Corinthians 5:8).

Q71. Where will believers spend eternity?
A71. Now I saw a new heaven and a new earth, for the first heaven and the first earth had passed away. Also there was no more sea. Then I, John, saw the holy city, New Jerusalem, coming down out of heaven from God, prepared as a bride adorned for her husband (Revelation 21:1-2).

On Rewards

Q72. If salvation is by grace, through faith, apart from works, why do good works?
A72. For the Son of man shall come in the glory of his Father with his angels; and then he shall reward every man according to his works (Matthew 16:27).

Q73. Did Jesus tell you to work for eternal rewards?
A73. "But lay up for yourselves treasures in heaven, where neither moth nor rust destroys and where thieves do not break in and steal" (Matthew 6:20).

Q74. When will believers be judged for their rewards?
A74. For we must all appear before the judgment seat of Christ, that each one may receive the things done in the body, according to what he has done, whether good or bad (2 Corinthians 5:10).

Q75. Does everyone get the same reward?
A75. If anyone's work which he has built on it endures, he will receive a reward. If anyone's work is burned, he will suffer loss; but he himself will be saved, yet so as through fire (1 Cor 3:14-15).

Q76. Does everyone get to rule with Christ?
A76. If we endure, We shall also reign with Him (2 Timothy 2:12a).

Q77. Will a believer who denies Christ rule with Him?
A77. If we deny Him, He also will deny us (2 Timothy 2:12b).

Q78. Can you lose your inheritance in the kingdom?
A78. Do you not know that the unrighteous will not inherit the kingdom of God? (1 Corinthians 6:9).

Q79. What should be your attitude towards rewards?
A79. Do you not know that those who run in a race all run, but one receives the prize? Run in such a way that you may obtain it (1 Corinthians 9:24).

On Spiritual Maturity

Q80. What are the two kinds of Christians?
A80. And I, brethren, could not speak to you as to spiritual people but as to carnal, as to babes in Christ (1 Corinthians 3:1).

Q81. Does God expect you to grow spiritually?
A81. Therefore let us leave the elementary doctrine of Christ and go on to maturity, not laying again a foundation of repentance from dead works and of faith toward God (Hebrews 6:1 ESV).

Q82. What are the two kinds of life that Jesus came to give?
A82. "I have come that they may have life, and that they may have it more abundantly" (John 10:10b).

Q83. How can you have abundant life?
A83. "Abide in Me, and I in you. As the branch cannot bear fruit of itself, unless it abides in the vine, neither can you, unless you abide in Me" (John 15:4).

Q84. What part of you is born again?
A84. That which is born of the flesh is flesh, and that which is born of the Spirit is spirit (John 3:6).

Q85. What kind of inner struggle does the born-again believer face?

A85. For I delight in the law of God according to the inward man. But I see another law in my members, warring against the law of my mind, and bringing me into captivity to the law of sin which is in my members. O wretched man that I am! Who will deliver me from this body of death? (Romans 7:22-24).

Q86. Can you grow in spiritual maturity by following rules and regulations?
A86. These things indeed have an appearance of wisdom in self-imposed religion, false humility, and neglect of the body, but are of no value against the indulgence of the flesh (Colossians 2:23).

Q87. How can you be spiritually transformed?
A87. And do not be conformed to this world, but be transformed by the renewing of your mind, that you may prove what is that good and acceptable and perfect will of God (Rom 12:2).

Q88. How do you renew your mind?
A.88. "Sanctify them by Your truth. Your word is truth" (John 17:17).

Q89. How would you summarize the heart of the Christian way of life?
A89. "So he answered and said, "'You shall love the LORD your God with all your heart, with all your soul, with all your strength, and with all your mind,' and 'your neighbor as yourself'" (Luke 10:27).

Q90. What does it mean to love your neighbor?
A90. "But I say to you who hear: Love your enemies, do good to those who hate you, bless those who curse you, and pray for those who spitefully use you" (Luke 6:27-28).

Q91. Is there a priority in whom you should love?
A91. Therefore, as we have opportunity, let us do good to all, especially to those who are of the household of faith (Galatians 6:10).

Q92. How can a husband love his wife?
A92. Husbands, love your wives, just as Christ also loved the church and gave Himself for her (Eph 5:25).

Q93. How can a wife love her husband?
A93. Wives, submit to your own husbands, as to the Lord (Ephesians 5:22).

Q94. How can a parent love his child?
A94. And you, fathers, do not provoke your children to wrath, but bring them up in the training and admonition of the Lord (Ephesians 6:4).

Q95. How can a child love his parents?
A95. Children, obey your parents in the Lord, for this is right. "Honor your father and mother," which is the first commandment with promise (Ephesians 6:1-2).

Q96. How can an employee love his boss?

A96. Bondservants, be obedient to those who are your masters according to the flesh, with fear and trembling, in sincerity of heart, as to Christ (Ephesians 6:5).

Q97. How can a boss love his employee?
A97. And you, masters, do the same things to them, giving up threatening, knowing that your own Master also is in heaven, and there is no partiality with Him (Ephesians 6:9).

Q98. How can you love orphans and widows?
A98. Learn to do good; Seek justice, Rebuke the oppressor; Defend the fatherless, Plead for the widow (Isaiah 1:17).

Q99. How can you love prisoners?
A99. Remember the prisoners as if chained with them—those who are mistreated—since you yourselves are in the body also (Hebrews 13:3).

Q100. How do you love church workers?
A100. Let the elders who rule well be counted worthy of double honor, especially those who labor in the word and doctrine (1 Timothy 5:17).

Q101. How often should you forgive others?
A101. Then Peter came to Him and said, "Lord, how often shall my brother sin against me, and I forgive him? Up to seven times?" Jesus said to him, "I do not say to

you, up to seven times, but up to seventy times seven" (Matthew 18:21-22).

Q102. How much money should you give to ministry?
A102. Every man according as he purposeth in his heart, so let him give; not grudgingly, or of necessity: for God loveth a cheerful giver (2 Corinthians 9:7).

Q103. How often should you pray?
A103. Pray without ceasing (1 Thessalonians 5:17).

Q104. What should you pray for?
A104. Be anxious for nothing, but in everything by prayer and supplication, with thanksgiving, let your requests be made known to God (Philippians 4:6).

Q105. Should Christians be lazy?
A105. For even when we were with you, we commanded you this: If anyone will not work, neither shall he eat (2 Thessalonians 3:10).

Q106. What is the fruit of the Spirit?
A106. But the fruit of the Spirit is love, joy, peace, longsuffering, kindness, goodness, faithfulness, gentleness, self-control. Against such there is no law (Galatians 5:22-23).

Q107. How should you react to adversity in life?
A107. My brethren, count it all joy when you fall into various trials, knowing that the testing of your faith

produces patience. But let patience have its perfect work, that you may be perfect and complete, lacking nothing (James 1:2-4).

Q108. What does God do to His children who sin?
A108. God disciplines us for our good, in order that we may share in his holiness (Hebrews 12:10b).

Q109. What should you do when you sin?
A109. If we confess our sins, He is faithful and just to forgive us our sins and to cleanse us from all unrighteousness (1 John 1:9).

Q110. If you confess your sins, what does God promise to do?
A110. He is faithful and just to forgive us *our* sins, and to cleanse us from all unrighteousness" (1 John 1:9b).

On the Church

Q111. What is another name for the church?
A111. Now you are the body of Christ and individually members of it (1 Corinthians 12:27 ESV).

Q112. Does your race, class, or gender matter?
A112. There is neither Jew nor Greek, there is neither slave nor free, there is neither male nor female; for you are all one in Christ Jesus (Galatians 3:28).

Q113. How were you made part of the Body of Christ?
A113. For by one Spirit we were all baptized into one body—whether Jews or Greeks, whether slaves or free—and have all been made to drink into one Spirit (1 Corinthians 12:13).

Q114. Does God want you to worship with other believers?
A114. Not forsaking the assembling of ourselves together, as is the manner of some, but exhorting one another, and so much the more as you see the Day approaching (Hebrews 10:25).

Q115. Do all church members have the same job?
A115. And He Himself gave some to be apostles, some prophets, some evangelists, and some pastors and teachers (Ephesians 4:11).

Q116. Do all church members have the same gifts?
A116. There are diversities of gifts, but the same Spirit (1 Corinthians 12:4).

Q117. What is a benefit of meeting with other believers?
A117. As each one has received a gift, minister it to one another, as good stewards of the manifold grace of God (1 Peter 1:10).

Q118. Who can participate in worship?
A118. Whenever you come together, each of you has a psalm, has a teaching, has a tongue, has a revelation, has

an interpretation. Let all things be done for edification (1 Corinthians 14:26b).

Q119. Should Christians eat together as a church?
A119. Now on the first day of the week, when the disciples came together to break bread (Acts 20:7a).

Q120. Is the Lord's Supper a real supper?
A120. And He took *bread*, gave thanks and broke it, and gave it to them, saying, "This is My body which is given for you; do this in remembrance of Me." Likewise He also took the *cup* after *supper*, saying, "This cup is the new covenant in My blood, which is shed for you" (Luke 22:19-20).

Q121. How often should you celebrate the Lord's Supper?
A121. "This do, *as often as you drink it*, in remembrance of Me" (1 Corinthians 11:25b).

Q122. What two things are you doing when you celebrate the Lord's Supper?
A122. "This do, as often as you drink it, in *remembrance* of Me." For as often as you eat this bread and drink this cup, *you proclaim the Lord's death* till He comes (1 Corinthians 11:25b-26, emphasis added).

Q123. What does baptism mean?
A123. Or do you not know that as many of us as were baptized into Christ Jesus were baptized into His death? Therefore we were buried with Him through baptism

into death, that just as Christ was raised from the dead by the glory of the Father, even so we also should walk in newness of life (Romans 6:3-4).

Q124. Who can be baptized?
A124. And many of the Corinthians, hearing, believed and were baptized (Acts 18:8b).

Q125. What can Christians do to discipline other members?
A125. But now I have written to you not to keep company with anyone named a brother, who is sexually immoral, or covetous, or an idolater, or a reviler, or a drunkard, or an extortioner—not even to eat with such a person (1 Corinthians 5:11).

On the Last Things

Q126. Will Jesus coming back?
A126. "Men of Galilee, why do you stand gazing up into heaven? This same Jesus, who was taken up from you into heaven, will so come in like manner as you saw Him go into heaven" (Acts 1:11).

Q127. Are we living in the last days?
A127. God, who at various times and in various ways spoke in time past to the fathers by the prophets, has in these last days spoken to us by His Son, whom He

has appointed heir of all things, through whom also He made the worlds (Hebrews 1:1-2).

Q128. What is the Tribulation?
A128. "For then there will be great tribulation, such as has not been since the beginning of the world until this time, no, nor ever shall be" (Matthew 24:21).

Q129. When does the Tribulation begin?
A129. Then he shall confirm a covenant with many for one week" (Daniel 9:27).

Q130. Will the Church go through the Tribulation?
A130. For God did not appoint us to wrath, but to obtain salvation through our Lord Jesus Christ (1 Thessalonians 5:9).

Q131. How will Jesus save the Church from the Tribulation?
A131. For the Lord Himself will descend from heaven with a shout, with the voice of an archangel, and with the trumpet of God. And the dead in Christ will rise first. Then we who are alive and remain shall be caught up together with them in the clouds to meet the Lord in the air. And thus we shall always be with the Lord (1 Thessalonians 4:16-17).

Q132. What happens to the Church after the Rapture?
A132. For we must all appear before the judgment seat of Christ, that each one may receive the things done in

the body, according to what he has done, whether good or bad (2 Cor 5:10).

Q133. What follows the Tribulation?
A133. And I saw thrones, and they sat on them, and judgment was committed to them. Then I saw the souls of those who had been beheaded for their witness to Jesus and for the word of God, who had not worshiped the beast or his image, and had not received his mark on their foreheads or on their hands. And they lived and reigned with Christ for a thousand years (Revelation 20:4).

Q134. What will life be like during the millennium?
A134. The wolf and the lamb shall feed together, The lion shall eat straw like the ox, And dust shall be the serpent's food. They shall not hurt nor destroy in all My holy mountain," Says the LORD (Isaiah 65:25).

Q135. How does the millennium end?
A135. Now when the thousand years have expired, Satan will be released from his prison (Revelation 20:7).

Q136. What will happen to Satan after the Millennium?
A136. The devil, who deceived them, was cast into the lake of fire and brimstone where the beast and the false prophet are. And they will be tormented day and night forever and ever (Revelation 20:9).

Q137. Where will millennial people be judged?

A137. Then I saw a great white throne and Him who sat on it, from whose face the earth and the heaven fled away. And there was found no place for them. And I saw the dead, small and great, standing before God, and books were opened. And another book was opened, which is the Book of Life. And the dead were judged according to their works, by the things which were written in the books (Revelation 20:11-12).

Q138. How will unbelievers be judged?
A138. And anyone not found written in the Book of Life was cast into the lake of fire (Revelation 20:15)

Q.139 Where will believers spend eternity?
A139. Now I saw a new heaven and a new earth, for the first heaven and the first earth had passed away. Also there was no more sea (Revelation 21:1).

Q140. What do we pray in the meantime?
A140. He who testifies to these things says, "Surely I am coming quickly." Amen. Even so, come, Lord Jesus! (Revelation 22:20).

Shawn Lazar (BTh, McGill; MA, VU Amsterdam) was born and raised in Montreal, Canada. He and his wife Abby live with their three children in Denton, TX. He writes and edits for Free Grace International (www.freegrace.in). His other books include:

- *Beyond Doubt: How to Be Sure of Your Salvation*
- *Chosen to Serve: Why Divine Election Is to Service, Not to Eternal Life'*
- *One-Point Preaching: A Law and Gospel Model*
- *Scripturalism and the Senses: Reviving Gordon H. Clark's Apologetic*
- *It Takes God to Be a Man: The Spiritual Theology of Major Ian Thomas*
- *The Five Points of Free Grace (forthcoming)*

Made in the USA
Columbia, SC
28 February 2024